M000301901

a recipe for...

Shruthi Dandamudi

All rights are reserved. No part of this book may be reproduced into a physical, electronic, or mechanical copy without permission from the author.

Copyright © Shruthi Dandamudi, 2021

All parts of this book, including pictures and graphics, were created by Shruthi Dandamudi.

A dedication to:

Kranthi and Rani Dandamudi,

Thank you for teaching me to strive confidently and love unconditionally.

To my readers,

I hope your journey through my words can help establish a path for your life in which you can walk through with clarity and confidence.

Chapters

Salt

For Change

-

I saw it a mile away

Like weather particles chasing

away fall to winter

My symptoms worsened as I

fell closer into a corpse I never

knew existed

My hair touched beneath shadows,

growing into adulthood

My emotions couldn't defeat fear

Fear was inevitable

Lurking in the corner of every hall I

needed to discover

I was lost in paved cement trying to

find myself

Trying to find qualities that were

pleasant surprises, gifts to souls

Trying to perform my morning duties

Rake all of the red, orange, blue, green

leaves away to prepare for the storm

to come

Make all color in the world invisible into a blank

slate to start over and

figure out what life really was

My thoughts encompassed terror

For hailstorms and nightmares to

drown me in the ground beneath me

Trying to guide my way through

a tunnel I couldn't see in

Through weather which was

only getting worse

Temperatures dropping

Flashlights leaving my vicinity

Trees telling me that they were

slowly preparing to die

It was my cue that I was facing

the real world, real issues with

nobody but myself

I didn't know how to deal with it

So did the world outside of me

So we decided to shut off

And hibernate into medicine capsules

For people to reuse again and again

and hope to be saved

Until Poseidon takes over

Decides that more is to

overcome us

I was still trying to figure out

why and when and how

He never gave me answers

It was just me against the

world and that's it

For a Fighter

-

I stand there

Letting the wind tremble over me

Blowing my ripened

petals away

And slowly deteriorating my insides

I stand there

And let it all happen

For I am not strong enough

to fight or flee

I stand there

Though I'm lucky to be

replenished every day

So my roots can take in the water

Flushing tension away

It is an endless cycle

A game called life

A game of ping-pong played

Knocking me out until I

ricochet off the wall and hit the ground so hard

Rolling off into a place unrecognized

A place where my bright pink

petals cannot take the tension

A place where my love weakens

and my body aches until it shrivels

I lay there to let myself pass

I lay there freely

Arms stretched out as

wide as they can be

Eyes closed

Crying for help

Screaming excruciating pain

Don't give up

Don't give up

Don't give up

I am too weak

I want to be a fighter

I want to embody all the

traits of her and her and her

I want to look as beautiful as her

Wants are not needs

What you want isn't always

what you need

I try to lift my fragile body up

slowly without sinking into

the dirty surroundings of

Mother Nature

The depths of this mysterious beauty

Able to arise greater than ever before

I learn and am still learning to accept

nothing but my one soul

With many cracks and ridges

With many areas to grow and develop

May not be the easiest to repair,

but will always be a part of me

and my bright pink petals

For Failing

-

In front of all of your successes

is a failure telling you to

let go of the ropes you've

been pulling to steer closer

to your dreams

Telling you that success will

never come upon you and

take you beyond your perception

Failure is a bold X that

can't be erased

Always recorded in your

history book

Taken from worst case scenarios

Failure was written last minute

when procrastination arrived

at your front doorstep

It is a sponge that absorbs

tension from sticky

surroundings

and releases the worst inside

of you

A narcissistic existence in our

minds which keeps us from

taking the leaps we had

imagined since we could walk

But what we didn't know is

that failure has a stop button

Timing out when its'

boundaries have been crossed

Anyone and everyone can

reach that stop button with their

bare hands and display the beast of a

burden that they conquered

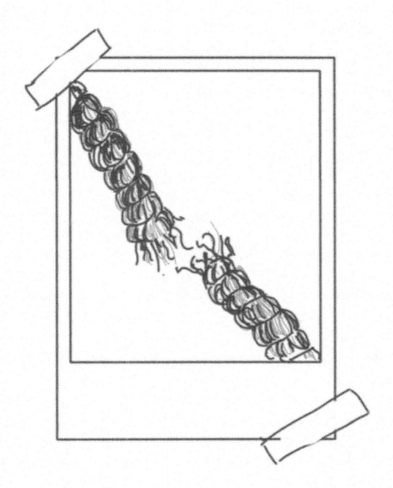

For Hate

-

These days I end up scrolling
my night away through
hourglass Hollywood figures
and social media hate captured
like bait

These nights I watch the hour
hand on the clock move like
lightning through white sheer
curtains as life becomes a
competition

I watch an endless movie as
society continues to sculpt
their picture perfect bodies

50 points for weight

50 points for looks

It can't all just be in one book

Graded on a rubric too rudely

Creatures of self destruction

and creators of mind manipulation

Face tuning and filtering is

never enough

My hand can't leave

the game we are playing to grab and go the next

meal to binge and regret afterwards

These nights anxiety peaks

where mountains become cold,

where my hand turns purple,

and deserts long for attention

And these days their business

becomes everyone's business

which becomes the world's

business

These days that meal is too

hard to digest, too immune to misery

Self love is preached upon

self destruction

Our hands become our weapons

Love becomes hate and

hate comes a cycle

These days the soil becomes

dirtier and grasses becomes drier

The sun shines dimmer and

waves crash slower

The rain showers harder and

sky becomes blacker

The stars vanish sight and

streets turn into empty roads

for people to use after they are

done with their game

For people to repost their next

"I wish" comment

These days the world never

ceases to change their perception

and wisdom

These days society is a competition

A built in simulation in our

minds to find the best candidate

But that was never right

Because life is never a competition

Stop the comparison within yourself

For Luggage

-

My backpack carried all the materials

I was using to develop a strong-weighted

hypothesis

Some days it held burdens and bricks

that I was unconfident to let go of

Some days my headaches never let

new thoughts enter and leave with ease

Some days I was leaping over hurdles,

finding new treasures to keep tucked away

But everyday I was willing to learn

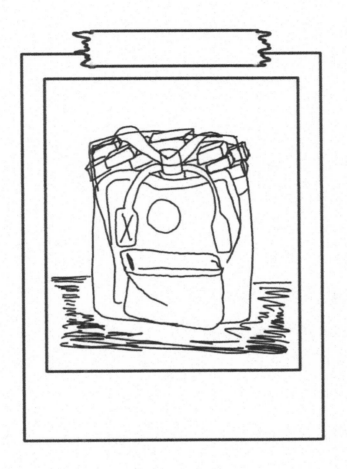

For Silence

-

Our silence is a storage bin

Swept under an ancient rug

A doormat, walked over

by people at anytime

Locked inside to save for reuse

Placed untouched outside

our personas

Through our own silence, we

can see ourselves wandering

off into woods darker than the ocean

Find ourselves building our

own shelters to defend our

own fresh skin from brutal nature

calls

Our silence is words that

trickle down our throats

and left inside for days to rot

Is where our internal systems

began to shut down no matter how many

times we try to restart

It shows prestige

How high we can keep our crowns for

the world to see us perfect

Emotions are against guidelines because

punishments include more than gashes and

the healing process is not easy

So it's just easy to keep quiet

Our silence is a Rosemary seed

Waiting to be sprouted from ground up

To grow into beauty to be accepted in the

world

Waiting to establish worth, a reason why

we were brought into this planet

We find ourselves salvaging through loose

ends we can't tie up

Trying to keep those rotten words from

spilling out because words can hurt

Strong enough to let the pain take us into

black rooms filled with fear

Rooms where window panes don't exist and

escaping is prohibited

Rooms where at last, silence can leave our mouths

circulating around and around our minds in the

same dark room

It was just our brain's way of manipulation

For Oceans

-

I'm jealous of how oceans can roam their

homes however they please

How freedom can consist of every breath

they take and how their sounds never make

noise louder than whistles

I'm jealous of how oceans have so much

unity

Their life is so put together with every

blemish covered so perfectly

And still, they serve a purpose for

every soul in their home

And with time, they leave and come back

to never disappoint

For Losing Hope

-

It would be a beautiful, happy ending

Walls magically painted in coats of silver

and gold

My pillows would be clouds

I would be treated like a queen if second guessing

and giving up weren't options

I would fall asleep onto heaven's

shoulder

Until I am woken up by an alarm of birds

chirping and trees rattling

For Walls

-

I run into concrete too often

Walls

Left and right

Up and down

I can't miss them

Yet I do

Thinking about my thousand page to-do list

I miss my steps too often

My presence is a present wrapped with a

pretty bow gifted as a time bomb inside

My mind was too busy keeping count of how

many minutes I had left

I never told myself to live in the moment,

that I'd be able to get through chaos

My mind never allowed moments for deep

breaths, for extra minutes I needed

Walls were those reminders

Reminding me that it is absolutely ok to run

out of storage

To take a break even in the midst of disaster

To give yourself company, hold your

hand to nurture the pain

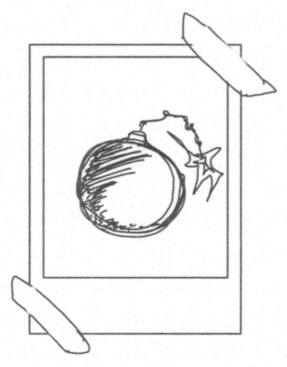

For Anxiety

-

When our hearts get heavy,

It feels like our throats have been

captured with so many lost hands who

never treated us with respect in the

first place

It feels like our lungs have been breathing

the same foul smoke that entered our

bodies right when our hands shook

the same hands as the ones who

captured us

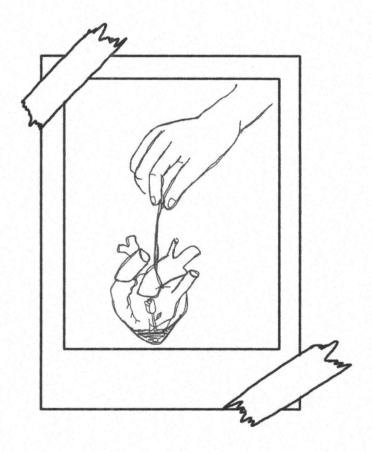

Ginger

For a Bruised Warrior

-

I can feel my flesh shrivel and burn into my soul
I can feel my skin deepen into my wounds as
I was a fighter struggling with post-war bruises
A victim and culprit of loss

My young years weren't like this I tell u
I was full with excitement in my soul and
energy reaching up so high I could touch the sky
My bones were rock solid and dense
And no post-war bruises were ever present

I grew up watching rainbows after rainstorms
and sunrises at 5 a.m
My aches were never pain
Pain was never a struggle

Struggle was never a burden on my shoulders

So heavy I can't keep myself up

So heavy the weight crushes me until I

am numb to the pain

Those nights of betrayal have lasted too long

Too late to repair these battle bruises

Now they've become scars that will never go away

Engraved on me like a signature

I'm not growing anymore

I've stopped growing

I'm not growing anymore

My bones are becoming fragile like glass that

is breakable

My body aches until it shivers

My fevers reach 105 degrees Fahrenheit

Side effects include nausea, vomiting, and

severe discomfort

My pain is always struggle

My struggle is always a burden

Burden too heavy to carry

Most days I can't see very clearly

No territory to claim my own

I'm still running this race at full speed

and can't catch up

I'm the last one still running

I'm still far from the finish line

But victory is in sight

Cheering me on to run a little faster

Victory tells me that the pain was

worth the journey

Pain was something that was supposed to

happen

That it will lead me to the finish line

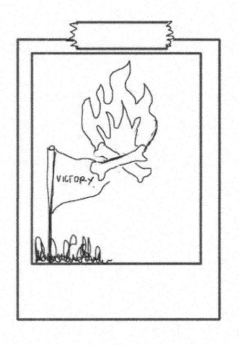

For Resilience: Realization

-

City lights hit home bright
Blood covered battlefields inevitable to live
Eat, sleep, breathe, repeat

Running across streets chasing after the
nearest grocery store filled to the brim with
chicken noodle soup or bread loaves and
peanut butter and jam
Only to fill your box of gratification on
your grocery list

Messing up your four serving dinner order
as an excuse to leave
Paying the price of thousands and thousands
just for yourself

Eat, sleep, breathe, repeat

For 24 minutes

24 hours

24 days

And reverse

Repeat, breathe, sleep, eat

Telling you to find your heart on the bottom

of your bedside table when you're hungry

Telling you that it wasn't worth it so that

your stomach shrivels up into a guilt

filled sanctuary

Reminding you that we do nothing but

wait for torches to be lit for guidance through

darkness

That you do nothing but make darkness darker

Telling you that it just wasn't worth it

Eyes with water covered puddles

Blood drenched faces

When realization hits

Telling you that self satisfaction was just a

threat to your own life

A trip to the ER

A trip you will never forget

A threat to thousands

A threat to your family

A threat to your friends and grandparents

and their mothers and fathers

Stop making us weaker

Digging holes that should've stayed

healthy grasses

Fresh flowers

Stop making excuses

They're just not worth it

Not right now

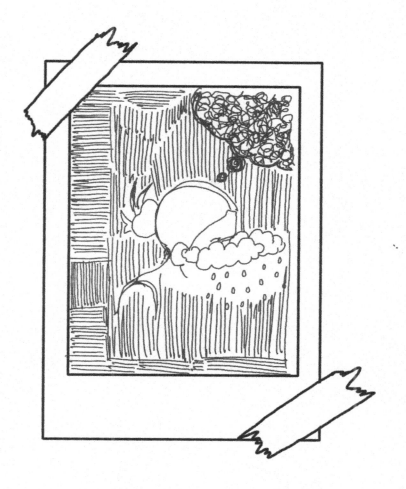

For Goodbyes

-

And in the wave of saying the last goodbye

The last tear was the hardest to watch

disappear into thin air

I spent hours trying to soak up the aftermath

into a jar, but I was too late

Because endings are so painful to let go of

And leave us earlier than we can

53

For Acceptance

-

Beauty is never good enough

Because we sculpt our airplanes so perfectly

And when they're time to fly, they crumble

in front of our faces

Vanishing the dreams we had built in our brains

Our goals we had hand drawn in our timelines

Like storybooks made from purity

Birds singing softly on their morning fly to

West Hampshire

Use Google as our savior weapon to find all

natural two ingredient recipes

All natural two meal diets

Because eating grass for lunch is good for you

And two grains of sugar will last you for two

weeks

Split the two into fourths and into thirds and

into fifths for maximum results

Starving our pitiless stomachs so they

become sad weeping stones hovering over

toilet seats

Yelling to get out of the trap that they were put in

They say beauty is pain but pain was never

meant to be as far as tears in dirty drains

And hearts on broken platters

Aimless emotions

Sad aromas where food never tastes the same

You lost too much fat you can't swallow back up

You ate too much so you can't carry yourself

up the stairs through your own skin

Into your own sanctuary

Your brain became two nonfunctional

pieces of meat for you to contemplate over

and over and over again

Caught comments that were always artificially

thrown together last minute

Your brain tried to catch clocks that can

escape our conscious and move life at a

pace of two hundred miles per hour

But you never told yourself to breathe

Reminded yourself to stop running and start

walking because that was all that was needed

For Defense

-

Most of the time, I can't take the tension of
candle smoke weathering off into the air to
be born into more polluted sites

Shuttering against my eyes through black and
white, my pupils only catch blankness in the
streams of white and gray
My face remains still
Even beneath tunnels
I care about clarity too much
All I can do is let my brain take over my voice
I can't move under a shell I can hide in
My only safe space
Where I can hibernate through five month
long winters to beat myself up over and over
again

The wells beneath me drain the water I
drink into sewage systems
Left my spirits lower than the force that
brought me to life

I'm scared of the world
My home
My movie is fast forwarding to infinite futures
Rummaging through times I was meant to
experience

My brain can't finish paragraphs of hate and
unwelcoming people that try to enter
It's hard for me to comprehend because I'm too
slow and just can't keep up

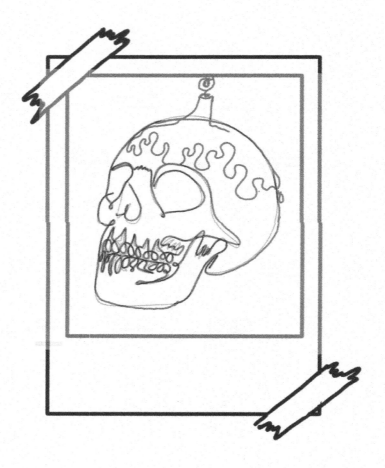

For Digital Connection

-

It wasn't meant to be taken to extreme lengths

Lengths that were farther than your

brain could imagine

Our world flipped upside down as I

snapped my fingers and so did love

Now spelled backward *e v o l*

Love is through a computer screen

Signaling reciprocation messages

All of a sudden our eyes could touch nothing

but computer screens with palms wanting to

work ways into the screens as if they were

time portals

It prohibited traveling, but trespassing hidden

grounds is all we wanted to do

Ride over clouds

The most beautiful part of it all was

taken away by thieves and snatched into

electronic machines

Withered away into awkward conversation

With no hesitation

But screens forced us to live in time, in the

moment where everything was taken and

we just had to improvise

Perform our improv routines

We were forced to grow our roots even longer

than they were before

Love wasn't meant to be challenged like this

Taken into burial sites and stored in open

caskets, with hope to revive back to life one day

It's almost like it was reborn, into a new human

with new qualities

Introducing isolation and deprivation as

front runners

It had to learn its' ways and techniques

Figure out this world

Adjust to updates and viruses

People had to trust the process

For Avocados

-

Something about avocados has always
fascinated me
How vulnerable something as small a
vegetable can be
It makes me question why humans, people
of thought, struggle to show true emotion
There's always a layer that can't be peeled
for most people
A layer that lies deep in our bodies which
is selfish enough to never come out
We can strip out every part and leave nothing
left of a vegetable, but when it comes time to us,
our presence does not exist
And yet an avocado could sit there, dictated
to meet our commands with no
incentive

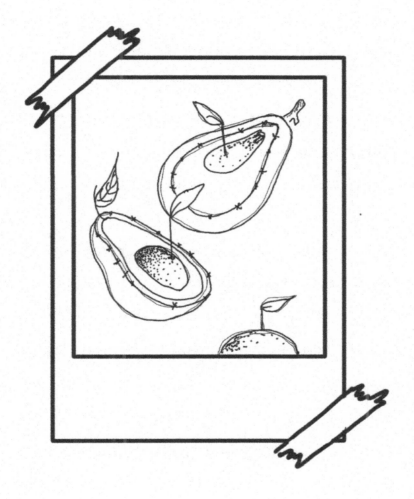

For Perfection

-

1. Get your bags and your keys, shove them
down your pockets and run out the door

2. Your worries and emotions should disappear
into your pockets
Tucked where they're unnoticed

3. Drive your bionic arms functioned to turn
right on Hell Street and left on God knows where

4. Don't drive too fast or your keys will fall into
bigger problems you never needed

5. Check yourself for indented skin and
over-lined lips
Remember the rest goes in your pockets
Slipped away into misery

6. Remove the bricks off your shoulders
because they can't see you work too hard to
carry too heavy of burdens

7. Make sure your pockets can carry the
weight from your own skin
Make sure you leave no dirty marks
Make sure your hair is pin straight
Make sure your pockets can fit
fifty pounds of weight
Make sure you have back up bodyguards
Make sure you make yourself second priority
Perfect pocket, perfect pocket, perfect pocket,
perfect pocket

8. When Laundry day arrives, hide your pants
into secret sanctuaries where no one can see your
hidden treasures

9. Hide them so vaguely you forget where they are

Find more pockets to fit more weight

Find pockets to flush tension through ripped

holes and onto weakened skin

Clenching your body so hard that veins leave trails

marks for help

Keep the cycle on repeat, cleansing your clothes

to compensate your dirty pockets

Repeat until your wardrobe is decorated

without pockets, hidden at plain sight

Lost through frustrations

Through guilt traps

No more pockets to hide the tension

Nothing can assist perfection

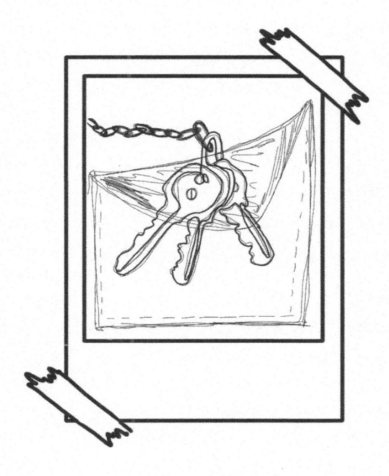

For the Future

-

I spent too many of my growing years trying to

sketch the perfect version of myself

I fell in love with a false picture with fake

ideas and folks

Trying to break the image was a long journey

It seemed surreal that it could go a different

way than I planned

And that my brain wasn't mentally prepared

for an alternate reality

But it's how my chapters turned and pages

were written

Turmeric

For Directions

-

I am lost

Trying to find my way through hurricanes

and flooding feet

Trying to find answers that were scribbled

over in sharpie

Through dirt and compost mixtures

Trying to navigate through an endless

journey of frustrations

Life never giving me enough lemons to make...

Lemons were never sour enough to make

juice sweeter than pie

But these aren't just lies

My reflection became blackness, that pushes

me deeper into indents

Blankets me, drowning me into my own skin

My GPS is broken saying *u-turn* ten thousand
times on repeat

I am lost
I can't find my way through rainstorms and
tilted landscape

I can't leave this ongoing dreamworld
I can't feel my emotions
Telling me to turn left
I can't let myself speak
I can't drive anymore
I am so lost at sea
Trying to find the nearest lifeboat
to save me
To become the best day of my life

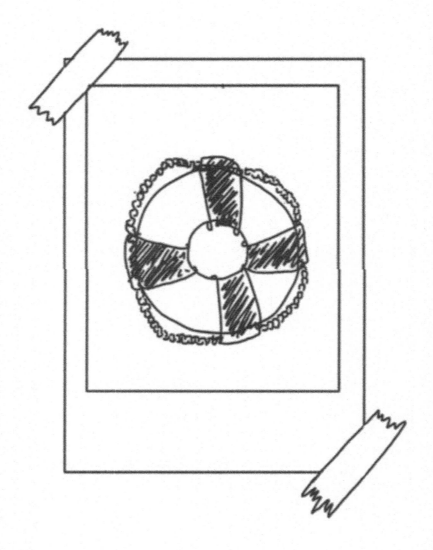

For My Roots

-

Sometimes I like to roam off into wonderlands

where I can picture where my destiny lies

Beneath hidden tracks or soft skies

I know I'm just in a game of hide and seek

Trying to find where everything is hidden

I know my founders carved out perfect quality

material

Held me with brave hands and nurtured

me through growing pains

Through times where physical strength was

no option

For Destiny

-

Destiny lies where my roots grow

Becomes strong and capable of the world

that I saunter through

A world where bravery is no second option

One which creates cuts on my feet unbearable

enough to bear

Taking lessons that were learnt to step in

different directions

I'm preparing for a long game of hide and seek

One that takes me through trials and tribulations

Through chaos and crime

Boldness and boredom

I'm trying to figure out my path

Never ending

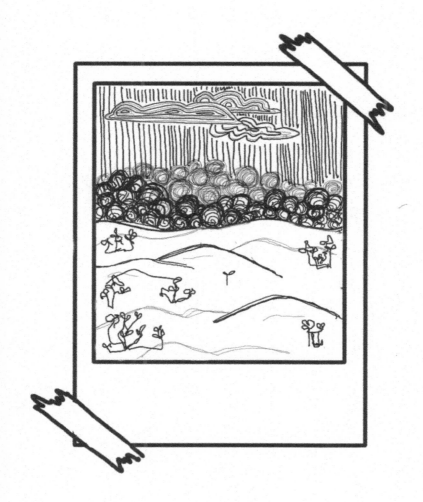

For Baby Breath

-

Opening my eyes for the first time felt like

being birthed into a world of color

A world that gave me the confidence to

discover new thoughts

To hold on to my mother's finger only to

exchange information about the love I had

kept in for so long in the womb

I could hear every whistle so clearly

I could, for the first time, show emotion

to the world and the world could reciprocate

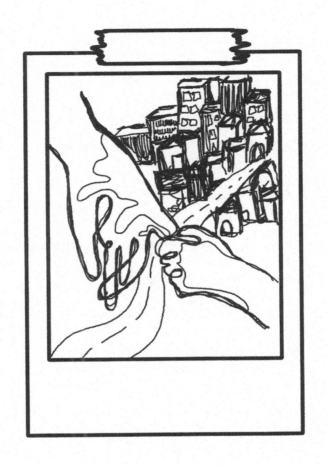

For My Territory

-

My country comes with peace
Dressed in bangles and blues
My country, not appreciated finds a way
to appreciate

Immigrants making their way through hurdles
and rainstorms in dark blue seas
Jumping bullets for cash and sweating gallons
for food
Handcuffed to speak the same language
Robot functioned to act the same way
Walk the same way
Talk the same way
Laugh the same way
Ride the same way

Error: further functions not provided

My country once protected in silk, ruined

by gas leaks and garbage

Do you work for I.T?

Support is never caved but craved for

Used like a pawn in a game of chess

Knocked out and killed, no second chances

Hiding our three course lunches because curry

looks like flavorless meat

Can I have your...

Homework that people never "understood"

and ripped bare bone until they got to school

What do you...

Speaking caused problems when mouths

moved to the rhythm of eye blinks

Moving caused damages that were camera

monitored

Breathing caused $300 fines

My country came with prize possessions

Earth found treasures

Life born victories

But that never mattered

That never mattered when uncle was out fixing

broken beams and aunty was planting seeds to

grow humans that will respect them

For Dodging Hurdles

-

My mind feels like a cannonball

Blows up when activated and quiet when

dysfunctional

Refilled with dark, metal bullets when needed

only to blow up when activated

What defines me is my beliefs

Fiery smoked balls which travel across the two

lobes trying to make the decision

on where to go and what to do

Until my brain can't choose the best option

My fear trickles into the very corner where

it can be accepted

Begging for the survival it needed

Building brick bone barriers barricaded

in the restricted area

I never knew what to believe

It was always the same bullets

Dark, metal

It was never anything different

Hope never made its' way around victory

My brain could never think about anything

else but the same bullets

Dark, metal

So dense and heavy

My brain could not handle anymore tension,

but I had to fight the war in which I was put in

It's now or never

I couldn't think about other options

I couldn't handle another activation which

would kick me to the outside territory

where I would drown in an ocean filled with filth

Middle of nowhere

No help

No helicopter

Just me and my hundred pound bullets

Dark and heavy

Which has shaped me into an independent

woman

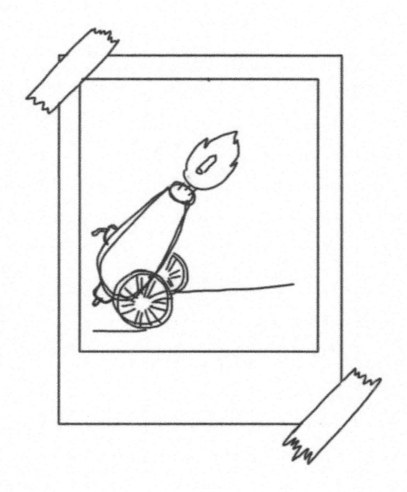

For Daisies

-

The earth is where I dwell

Shriveled stems storming from pots to be plants

Moments were never mistakes but melting points

where everyone decided to put their finger in at

 once and burn off twice

My shadows long for attention

Craving for my skin to grow into long bodied

models

The earth told me he wanted uniformity

White, delicate daisies and nothing more

Strong stemmed masculinity

No shapes were accepted

He told me to leave if I wasn't one of those

He held my throat in his hands so tightly

threatening my existence

Petals weathered off into pots if they weren't white
and long

He told me I wasn't meant to be nurtured by the
other daisies

The fabric upon my skin was never meant to be
black because uniformity wasn't written across it,
double stamped, with his approval

He's harsh sometimes

The expectations are an ongoing list of lessons I
should learn from

Perfect is where I should have come from

Perfect bodied

Pink lips

Pretty waist

My hands can't leave my world

My earth

He is an addiction

He slurps me into traps I can't get out of

Created in cotton ball clouds and gradient sunsets
I am commanded by him to listen to his demands
or else my water will turn into salty rivers that
aren't drinkable
Blonde hair and blue eyes was what he wanted
It was what they all wanted

All the other little daisies galloping in the field
with their long stemmed bodies and white faces
They joined in uniformity, so happy while I sat in
the corner shriveled up, waiting for freshwater to
reach my soul and give me nutrients that would
help me grow

My living situation isn't clean right now
I'm weak and old with health conditions and can't
live up to his critical comments
They hurt

They feel like slaps on my face a hundred beats per
second

The earth himself is turning into a

needy and demanding monster

My so called world is a dark chamber

A jail cell I can't get out of

He wishes me bad luck

But I can't live without him

For Trips

-

Society has expectations
Things to abide by
And these things take us on trips across the world
just to gain no outcome

Trips that are so costly
These trips are where inspiration boards are black
papers waiting to be written on
I often find myself lurking through Paris and Rome
just to find five star restaurants for my perfect
life
I find myself planning beyond my ages
Throwing proud moments into the past
Leaving reapers to grow seeds
Even for the eternities after me
My pages skip too fast

Galloping with the wind to seek acceptance

Closing off chapters I shouldn't have closed and

disregarding opportunities I should've taken

I drew culture away like it was a beast

And dressed myself in the finest jewelry in stock

I never stopped myself to live in the moment

I was too busy trying to take a step in every

corner of the world but my own home

For Wings

-

I've always wanted to become a fairy as a little girl

Not the kind that you can dress up as for a day but

the kind that can fly through shadows and more

Peeking through spirits and bodies

I've dreamed that, one day, I could visit heaven if

my key allows me to

And the wings i've been sculpting in my mind for

so many years could cherish every hand hold my

grandpa used to call *evening walks*

I wish, in another dimension, that wings worked

like I was taught magic did

How I could feel invincible from the rest of the

world, with no worries whatsoever

Wings could give me peace that my creation could be placed on my lap, handing me the validation I wanted

For Broken Pieces

-

I was left with broken glass pieces to clean up the
mess from somebody else's mistakes

Dead roses and ash clumped in my hands
reminded me of the sacrifices I had to make
Leaving me with cuts from the glass that weren't
fixable

I was too caught up trying to figure out ways to say
no
There just wasn't a button I could push for no
My lips could only touch *y*, *e*, and *s*
Utter the words of dread on repeat until my
function became simultaneous
Rooms were decorated with shattered glass
Dust bins waiting for their existence to make use
for trash day

It became a daily dilemma

Where my coffee spills became second priority

until the smell rotted like dead mice trapped in

the midst of trying to find homes

I wasn't made to be a servant

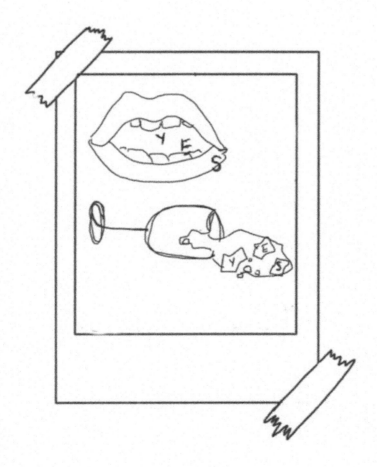

Honey

For Pleasures

-

You keep me sane when I'm not supposed to be
Smile against sad lips

You're the beach bay side where I spend my
spring, summer, and winter vacation
My every day
You're the corner side block party I will never stop
visiting
The drain tears flow past quietly
And something about you makes sadness feel ok
Makes insanity feel like normality
Makes my body a temple
Drenching myself in gold and smoke to cover up
my battle wounds
Cleanse my brain so that I can exfoliate my rigid
thoughts

Makes ancient tunes feel like a breath of fresh air

in a brief afternoon stroll with Gramps

You make self destruction absent

Which I can mark off the roll sheet everyday

To sit by my friend *Feliz* in Spanish class

Water tastes better when I'm in such golden

sanctuary because I'm numb to pain

Time freezes and that history test I have

tomorrow doesn't exist

The hours of creating my procrastination

schedule in my head for tomorrow morning does

not exist

My perfect future life page in my bullet journal

with pretty calligraphy font does not exist

An expectation does not exist

That happy ever after in that dreamworld Disney

movie will never exist

You are the only party I want to be invited to

You are my nightly ritual that I will never

forget to pray to

You are my zen meditation hour on high

grounds with mountain view

You are my happy place

I will grow old with you

But you will be new to me everyday

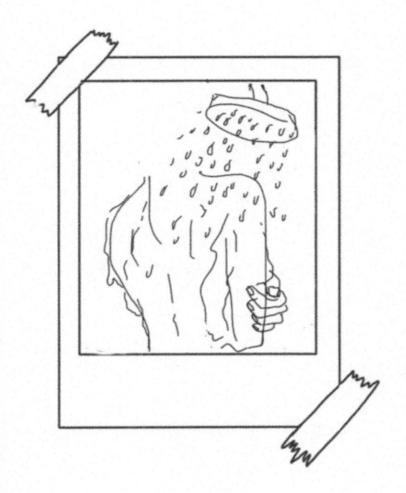

For Love

-

We give too much

For it's not easy to let go of the palaces we've

constructed inside our bodies

We let ourselves free of shields too often

Hike up prohibited territories

Force ourselves to live in extreme climates

Where danger could cave closer than we've ever

seen

We do whatever it takes to never let go of what our

intuition tells us

Try to send away help packages because of anger

Our hearts are so full one minute and the

next, a victim of destruction

For Blank Canvases

-

One day I was thrown into a room with all white
walls and told to make color in an empty void
which shouldn't exist anymore

To mix all the colors in the world the way that
emotions aligned with joy so perfectly
The way that beauty could be written in bold
letters across the shriveled vicinity

My fingers touched every ounce of cracked paint
cans trying to escape the trap that they've been
put in
Trying to become prisoners who escaped their
punishment homes

They've been raised on tunnel vision

Been raised inside jars to hide in silence, never

show emotion

It's been too long since they've seen light and it's

been too long since the world has seen color

I guess it's like a reunion

Where girl meets boy or people see each other

again for the first time after ten years

Pure happiness

It's like this sensation that can only be felt in a

certain situation

Like cold water hitting your skin for the first time

on a hot summer day

Their touch, so soft next to each other

It's almost what the world needed to revive itself

back to life

In the midst of all the chaos, paint was a
reminder that blank canvases were meant to be
salvaged from grave yards and brought to life

Paint was an afterlife medicine
It could bring the old back to life making age
subtract back in time
Designing my room into a colorful world

For Regrets

-

Every part of me tried not to choose patience

Tried to rip apart the thoughts in my head that

told me to conquer every moment of defeat

Tried to catch every voice that trickled down my

throat trying to make room for digestion

Every part of me had the confidence to drag myself

out of bed everyday with regret from yesterday

And leap through life like a fast forwarded song

With no pauses

Every part chose to hold on to the withered

artifacts that still remind me of my past

What I couldn't see was the garden waiting for me

to make way through a world full of life

For Reconstruction

-

She took the world's hand with such
confidence giving all her trust to the
guardians surrounding her

She new she was stepping into tulip gardens
and a happy Mother Nature
She new her beauty could be reciprocated
by the sky's emotions, sunrise and sundown

But when she fell into a trap with
comments that circulated in a black room
like false testimonies
She felt like the world gave back the
hand she had given it
That the work she had tirelessly spent hours
preparing for was scraped away into a ward

That the sky was grieving from loss and the only
option from saving itself was hurting others
She took harsh comments heavily, held
them on her shoulders weeping day after day
Her reflection became a devil to attack her
internal being

She couldn't look at herself the way she
did when she was held in arms of her
own comfort

She couldn't wake up at 5 a.m anymore to wish the
sunset good morning
She couldn't see the sky fully lit by the moon at
night
She couldn't hear the stars have conversations
about their love stories

She felt that the world was grieving, in a
messy way
She couldn't understand what was happening
Something needed to change and she broke
down the trap she fell so deep into, called up
her wishing well for help to visit therapist office
hours
Her tension was wiped away with healing and no
heartache and for the first time, everything came
full circle
Where she was now the world, taking the
hand of a young women which was once her

For Bubblegum

-

The thought of newness enters our systems so
excitingly
In the moment our anger and weak spots rush
away leaving room for nothing but contentment
Until used day after day on repeat like an alarm
Our minds train ourselves for what comes and
leaves

Knowing what everything entails
Routinely
Those emotions before the newness start trickling
back
The excitement washes away to scare our minds
Nothing but demons trying to get in our heads
It was just a test of approval
That anything can test our emotions

And we stand on the same grounds as yesterday

knowing our worth

For Never Letting Go

-

Today is the day
Tell them you love them
Kiss them goodnight
Breathe in confidence and breathe out the
message you have wanted to give for eternities
Cherish every hand hold

Tell them that you're thankful
For every ounce of joy that they hand delivered

Chase your feelings until outcomes are reached
Hold on to every page in your pocket
And don't let moments wither away from your
eyes
Because today is the day

For the Underworld

-

I wake up to a world of empty as I stare off

into the eyes of Poseidon

Look around and find blue stoned rocks and

green seaweed turning themselves into swords

to fight to stab all in sight

I can feel my weight sinking me deeper

down into darker blue thoughts

I can feel my lungs fill with fire and smoke

waiting to explode and turn into ashes

because I was put in these uncharted territories

and forced to live in darkness

I can see the the minute hand on the clock lapsing,

making its way around its'

evening jog in the colosseum that was built years

ago

The concrete is strong enough to peel my layers
apart and tell me I wasn't built like a god to cast
spells in wishing wells
No matter how hard I push I can't get out
I can't breathe in this broken building
I can't get out
Trying to mark my tracks as a call for help
No one.
Just an empty room trying to make conversation
with me
Distracting me from conquering
Stopping me from caving

No matter how hard I try, my body will be the
preeminence it enjoys
My feet are purple and stubborn to the same
thoughts on repeat

But I can still feel the softness of waves and

stillness of life telling me that it will be ok

I can still see cotton ball skies and glimpses of

fall leaves wandering off into their own homes

I can still picture my sanctuary just like yesterday

as it will never cease to leave my conscious

ATTACK- ATTACK- ATTACK

His army tries to skin my meat and thrash me

into weathered compost

The ocean floor becomes a black hole, rigid

with cracks as my legs fall deeper into this

ancient "palace", but my brain triggers

me that I am taking triumph

My thoughts gaze off into the currents of tides

only a hundred feet above me

I can do it

We can do it

And my army saves me of blood and gashes, close

to death

Bandaged me from enemies

I did it

We did it

Made impossibility a reality

For Gifts

-

Love is a gift

Wrapped up in layers with a pretty bow

Not just any kind of love but the love you find so

rarely

The love that makes you work for your desires

One that takes you down many boxes

The love that tingles every nerve in your body

Love makes you feel livid and happy and crazy

and excited to be holding something so precious

in your hands everyday

For 2020

-

You took away months of pride supposed to be
spent in gleaming castles composed of memory
jars to fill to the brim

You stored happiness under a dark rug
Waiting for hell to reach every crevice of...
This earth wasn't meant to be green and blue but
black all over
And we fought until victory be shun in light of
your presence

Your presence, an awful disguise wanted nothing
but pity
Just a chance in the spotlight
You were jealous of history books being written as
lighting ages

You made sure to cherish every tear you drank

with such dignity

And with time, you praise you will live for years

and beyond and the lives you have killed

Your wishes are certainties that

you add to your mind's timeline

Rejection was never a question

Your pupils never caught a glimpse of defeat, but

what you didn't know was the preparation

your opponents were making for your killing

For a day that your damage will be constructed

into buildings where you will be walked over

Six feet below and up

Your grave will become a dark hole perfectly

sculpted to fit your destiny

You didn't know the days we took building an army

of infinite members from every one you took

from us

But you taught us to live in the moment

That this life was meant for everyone but you

Everyone who walked the grounds in which they

wish were above you

Your lessons consisted of loving unconditionally

Even if that meant sacrificing what we never

wanted to

Your lessons told us that patience should never be

forgotten

a recipe for... is a selection, written in chapters, that explores the message that there are so many parts to an individual that makes them whole. There are so many ingredients that have to be combined to formulate a solution that satisfies all needs. Every individual will go through suffering and change to teach them many lessons. Through the process, they will learn to nurture every ingredient that comes their way with love and great compassion. Growth comes in increments of happy, pivotal, detrimental, and sad moments in life.

Growth is good. Failure is good. To keep a balanced journey, one must follow all the necessary steps to establish a healthy recipe for what creates them.

About *Shruthi Dandamudi*

-

Shruthi Dandamudi started writing in middle school with the help of her wonderful literature mentor, Mr. Dana Cleaborn. It quickly became something that came naturally to her. More seriously, her passion picked up in high school when she joined her school's poetry club in ninth grade. Because she was able to have an amazing poetry club sponsor and leader, Mrs. Sandrella Bush, she found herself writing and performing selections she never knew she could execute. Furthermore, she received many opportunities to be featured on national publications. Through rejection and acceptance, she knew poetry was something that would be close to her heart forever. *a recipe for...* started in her bedroom after a long day of work. She put together a collection of original writings and built on it later by writing more consistent selections. *a recipe for...* is a selection that she has worked tirelessly to perfect. She explores the themes of hardship, failure, growth, love, difference, and acceptance. She wants people to read this story and understand the importance of self-love as well as nurturing all of the sides of oneself. As a motivated high school student, she is proud of what she has accomplished and hopes to touch many souls through her work.